D1217760

Signature Solos

9 All-New Piano Solos by Favorite Alfred Composers

Selected and edited by **Gayle Kowalchyk**

Students love getting new music, and teachers love teaching it! What could be more fun than a book of new solos by several favorite Alfred composers? This collection of piano solos was expressly written for the *Signature Solos* series. A variety of different musical styles is found in each of the books.

As editor of this collection, it was a joy for me to play through many solos to find just the right grouping of pieces for each book. I looked for appealing sounds while considering the technical and musical abilities of students at each level. Students are sure to enjoy playing these "signature solos" for friends and family, informally or on recitals.

Gayle Kowalchyk

Alfred Music
P.O. Box 10003
Van Nuys, CA 91410-0003
alfred.com

ISBN-10: 1-4706-3217-9
ISBN-13: 978-1-4706-3217-5

Cover Photo
Colored Pencils: © iStock. / Adam Smigielski

All Is Calm

Dennis Alexander

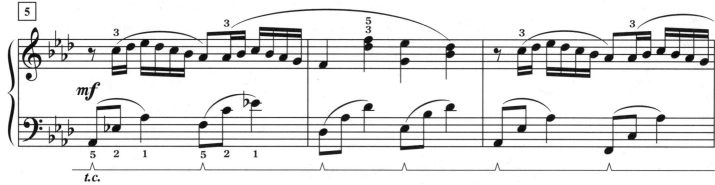

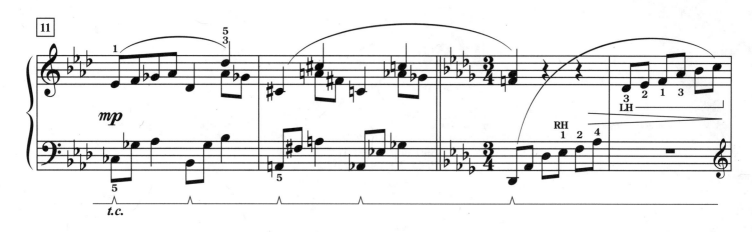

Rockin' Hard

Tony Caramia

A Song for Megan

W.T. Skye Garcia

Echoes from the Past

Martha Mier

Moderato con espressione

for Jonathan

Ghost Fantasy

Judy East Wells

Graceful Waltz

Melody Bober

15

for Heidi

Blue Kiss: A Lullaby

Christopher Brennan

* Smaller hands may delete the lowest note in the octave.

Shadowbrook

Kathy Holmes

for Caleb Michael Kuphall

Sunset Nocturne

Lee Galloway